TO:

FROM:

THE NIGHT BEFORE
COLLEGE

by Sonya Sones and Ava Tramer
illustrated by Max Dalton

Grosset & Dunlap
An Imprint of Penguin Group (USA) LLC

GROSSET & DUNLAP
Published by the Penguin Group
Penguin Group (USA) LLC, 375 Hudson Street, New York, New York 10014, USA

USA | Canada | UK | Ireland | Australia | New Zealand | India | South Africa | China

penguin.com
A Penguin Random House Company

Text copyright © 2014 by Sonya Sones and Ava Tramer. Illustrations copyright © 2014 by Max Dalton.
All rights reserved. Published by Grosset & Dunlap, a division of Penguin Young Readers Group,
345 Hudson Street, New York, New York 10014.
GROSSET & DUNLAP is a trademark of Penguin Group (USA) LLC.
Manufactured in the U.S.A.

Library of Congress Control Number: 2013016500

ISBN 978-0-448-46147-2   10 9 8 7 6 5 4 3 2

Dedicated to Bennett and Jeremy,

as per their request.

With love,

SS and AT

'Twas the night before college,
and from East Coast to West,
all the soon-to-be freshmen
could simply not rest.

As they tossed and they turned
by the moon's gentle light,
they were thinking of all
that had led to this night . . .

They had aced it in preschool,
read books by age four.
And before they turned six,
they had joined the Peace Corps.

By nine, they'd discovered
some new Mayan ruins.
By twelve, they'd been courted
to play for the Bruins.

By the time they reached high school,
there was no turning back—
they were headed for college.
Onward! Attack!

They were marching-band maestros,
en pointe in ballet.
They were master debaters,
virtuosos with clay.

They cleaned up the beaches.
They fed all the needy.
They sang for the old folks,
made gardens less weedy.

Though they'd worked their poor butts off,
it had prepped them so well
for applying to college—
The Process from Hell.

At the very beginning,
it wasn't that bad,
leafing through pamphlets
with Mom and with Dad.

Then they spent their spring breaks
taking tour after tour,
expanding their wardrobes
with campus couture.

PROUD PARENT
OF A COLLEGE STUDENT

They visited Rutgers,
then on to Purdue!
Now UMass! Now Georgetown!
Now Kalamazoo!

On Baylor! On Harvard!
On UNLV!
Now Berkeley! Now UConn!
Now ICUP!

They slept in the dorm rooms.
They sat in on class.
They talked with professors,
played Frisbee on grass.

They picked safeties and likelies
and also some reaches.
Then summertime came and . . .

They flocked to the beaches.

They soaked in the sun
and tried hard to relax,
but their pestering parents
wouldn't get off their backs.

"Work on your applications!
Put down that phone!"
"You're not the boss of me!
Leave me alone!"

Then fall was upon them,
and with classes resuming,
there was no time for stalling—
those deadlines were looming.

At SAT classes
each Saturday morn,
they bit off their nails,
wished they'd never been born.

'Cause they feared if they froze,
and the scores they got sucked,
the rest of their lives
would be totally . . . ruined.

On the day of the test,
they tried not to freak,
but the questions kept swirling—
it all looked like Greek!

"If only that girl
would stop cracking her gum . . ."
"If only that guy
would stop sucking his thumb . . ."

And then—hallelujah!
They heard "Pencils down!"
They sighed with relief
and went out on the town.

But their break was short-lived.
It ended that night,
when their parents screamed out,
"You've got essays to write!"

In just five hundred words,
could they tell their whole story,
of setbacks and hardship,
of triumph and glory?

Should they write about
saving their pet hamster's life?
Or what they learned from that cactus
about handling strife?

With their apps all submitted,
their FAFSAs all done,
and their transcripts all posted,
they were desperate for fun.

But then came the interviews.
They tried hard to enthrall.
Though they feared that they'd made
no impression at all.

And now
the most hideous phase would begin—
the waiting to find out
where they'd gotten in.

They stared at their laptops,
full of hope, full of fear,
when what to their wondering eyes
should appear,

but a whole bunch of e-mails
that caused them to smile—
"We are pleased to inform you . . ."
It had all been worthwhile!

They were itching to leave,
though they'd miss their dear folks,
hanging out with their friends,
and their siblings' lame jokes.

"Twas the night before college,
and all through the land,
the soon-to-be freshmen,
with teddies in hand,

dreamed of dorm rooms
and parties and clinking beer glasses,
and a couple of nerds
even dreamed of their classes.

All the luggage was set
by the front door with care.
They could hardly believe
that they soon would be there . . .

"T was the night *after*
the night before college,
and the freshmen were working real hard
to gain knowledge.

The way things were going,
their futures looked bright.

Happy college to all,
and to all a good night!